HEALING
from
EMOTIONAL
ABUSE

A PERSONAL JOURNEY THROUGH A TOXIC RELATIONSHIP

WAYNE ROTHMAN

Healing from Emotional Abuse: A Personal Journey Through a Toxic Relationship

WayneRothman.com

Publishing services provided by  Archangel Ink

Disclaimer

ISBN-13: 978-1-68965-480-7

DEDICATION

The problem with reading dedication pages is that books are always dedicated to someone else, never YOU.

Even though we haven't met, and may never meet, we have a great deal in common.

This book is for YOU.

YOU – who suffered years of emotional abuse and emotional confusion.

YOU – who are still struggling within an emotional relationship.

YOU – who came to accept that you are not to blame for your partner's behaviour.

YOU – who realised your relationship had to change.

YOU – who walked away from a toxic relationship.

We are fighting different battles within the same war, but will emerge stronger and wiser.

ACKNOWLEDGEMENTS

To my editor, Monica Muller - You took my words, worked your magic, and removed all the sharp edges so that my story could be read, understood and internalised by others.

To my brother Ian for agreeing to read my first draft and seeing something within the mess. A special thank you for introducing me to Monica.

To everyone who could only listen as they knew there was nothing they could do to help me along my journey.

CONTENTS

INTRODUCTION

Those of us who have been part of an emotionally abusive relationship will have had varied experiences.

The mechanics may be the same in many instances, but the dynamics will differ from relationship to relationship.

Whether you are a male or female victim of this form of abuse, you are in for a bumpy ride at the whims of your abuser unless you take control of the situation.

Once you realise you are being emotionally abused, you need to get out of the relationship as quickly as you can.

There is no other solution.

One thing I can say with utmost certainty is that most emotional abusers are incapable of changing their behaviour. For you to attempt to try and convince them to do so is a total waste of your time and energy.

If your abuser manages to pull you into their games and sees that you are a willing participant, you will suffer intensely for many years before you realise what is going on.

You are going to try and be patient and understand 'what they are going through' in the hope that they will eventually stop treating you in this manner.

You are going to look for excuses to justify their behaviour to those around you.

You will come to believe that what you are experiencing is quite normal and acceptable.

I don't believe there can be a single reason to justify the behaviour of an emotional abuser. As you read through this book, you will come to understand my reasons.

Due to patriarchal taboos, men have a difficult time admitting they too can be victims of emotional abuse.

Everything that has ever been written of males emotionally abusing females holds true in the opposite.

Let's be clear on one point; if you feel you are being emotionally abused by your partner, you probably are.

Doubting your instincts will be the cause of you enduring many years of emotional abuse.

I managed to 'escape' five years after entering into the relationship.

My ex-partner up to the point of publishing this book, still does not leave me in peace even though we live apart and have been doing so for almost eight years.

Emotional abusers are master manipulators, and as such, are an extremely treacherous group of individuals. You will find yourself questioning your value system, and may also make decisions along the way that, in hindsight, will shake you to your core.

They will challenge your sanity, and if you are not strong enough to cope with this, you will find yourself emotionally and financially scarred for life.

If there is only one piece of advice you take from this entire book, it must be that you walk away from an emotionally abusive relationship as soon as possible. Don't use anything as an excuse to keep yourself committed to the relationship. If there are children involved, fight for your kids from the onset, however difficult this may seem to be.

I need to point out that for a vast majority of the time that we were a couple, we lived apart.

Understand that what I have written here occurred mostly as a long-distance relationship. Work commitments dictated that I spent most of my time separated from a normal home life rather than living under the same roof as my partner.

I have used conversations we had through email and SMS's as examples throughout this book. Please be aware that some of the language used from these communications may be a bit harsh.

I am not a doctor or psychiatrist, nor do I hold a professional counselling degree.

What is written here is from personal experience, and are my own thoughts and conclusions.

1

WHAT IS EMOTIONAL ABUSE?

There are many definitions I can list for emotional abuse, but there is more to it than a simple set of words written by someone who may or may not have been involved in a relationship of this type.

It is more important to me that we understand what we are going through as it happens, not after the fact.

To come up with a definitive definition of emotional abuse is difficult as many other behaviours can, and do, form part of this type of ill-treatment.

Within any relationship, many factors influence the emotional interaction between partners.

Verbal abuse along with the financial aspects of the relationship, as well as using sex as a weapon, all have an emotional component attached to them, and these actions need to be part of the ultimate definition of emotional abuse we come up with.

The major issue in defining this form of abuse comes down to the question of why someone who supposedly loves you has this uncontrollable need to keep you feeling at your worst.

Also, why do you allow this to continue even after you become aware of the fact that you are being abused emotionally?

Therefore, to define emotional abuse, you have to take aspects from both sides, that of the abused and the abuser, and create a common ground.

I think the best way to define emotional abuse is the systematic breakdown of your soul by your partner over a protracted period.

It is not a once-off occurrence, it is very subtle and can go on for many years.

It is a pattern of behaviour on their part that digs so deep into your being that you eventually forget who you are, and come to believe that the only function you have is to please your abuser.

This form of abuse consists mainly of verbal innuendos that are layered on you and includes the repetition of incidents within your relationship such as humiliation, threats and even their favourite, the silent treatment.

It is a power game, and your abuser will attempt to mould you into becoming the person they want you to be; someone who is there for the sole purpose to satisfy whatever need they may have.

As long as they achieve their ultimate goal, which is to dominate and have total control over you, they are oblivious to how their behaviour affects you.

There are many tactics abusers use to get you to do their bidding, and we'll go through some of them as we progress through this book.

There are three main areas of emotional abuse you will start noticing after a period of time.

Firstly, your abuser will try to make you fearful of them and their behaviour, then deny any knowledge of them behaving in this manner, and finally, they will try and convince you that what is happening within the relationship is normal.

They are going to attempt to keep you in a state of emotional confusion.

A direct result of this poignant disorder is two questions that you will ask yourself repeatedly:

- Who is this person I am in a relationship with?
- Who am I? I don't recognise this person that I have become.

You will never know exactly where you stand with your partner; fire and ice come to mind.

The sad truth is that this cycle of behaviour is such a part of their makeup, that when they deny any knowledge of what they are doing, they believe what they are saying.

When we go into a relationship with someone we love, the one thing we are not afraid to do is to express this love verbally. 'I love you' was the last thing that crossed my lips each night before we went to sleep.

When my ex said the same words, they would usually come out as 'I love you too, but…'

It automatically put me on the defensive. I had that feeling that this may be the day she decides to walk away from our relationship.

There is always the subtle threat that they are in control and that they can leave at any time, even though this will never happen.

The woman I fell in love with never demonstrated any manipulative characteristics while we were in our 'getting-to-know-you' phase.

Or did she?

Was she so good at manipulating me that I didn't even notice what was happening from the moment we met?

I can now answer that question with a definitive YES!

I can't tell you how many times I was guilt-tripped into giving her what she wanted, even though this went against my better judgment.

I can't tell you how many times I did things to my detriment so that she could get what she was demanding from me.

By the time I realised what was happening, years down the line, it was too late.

I was so deep into the relationship that it felt I was a prisoner in my mind.

Your own life will take a back seat in your relationship.

Accepting emotional abuse is your reaction to behaviour that may cause you psychological trauma.

When someone treats you as though they don't care, don't even think that this is not the case.

You are going to be involved in a relationship where you are going to see two distinct fields of behaviour; that of your abuser and that of your own.

Your behaviour is always going to be treated as being on the wrong side of the equation.

You are always at fault, wrong, the attacker or flawed.

They are always blameless, right, the victim or perfect.

Anger is something else that is going to be a regular part of your daily emotional ride.

It doesn't matter what you contribute to the relationship: it is never enough.

I gave my everything, but it was never enough. There was always something that I did or said that made it my fault as to where my ex-partner found herself.

As this form of abuse is internalised, it will invariably lead you to become co-dependent on your partner.

I fell in love with her, and she was pretending to love me to get what she wanted.

There is only one certainty with an emotional abuser; they walk into a relationship with a game plan in mind - total power and control over you.

Don't believe for one second that you can have a normal relationship with someone who is emotionally abusing you.

2

CHARACTERISTICS OF AN EMOTIONAL ABUSER

An emotional abuser is the worst type of person you can ever come into contact with.

The longer you find yourself in an emotionally abusive relationship, the easier it will become to notice certain patterns of behaviour in your abuser.

This conduct seems to indicate that your abuser is in a mental conflict with themselves and those of us who have suffered at their hands are just victims of their abuser's deficiencies.

With what I have experienced in my relationship, I can attest to the fact that an emotional abuser has something amiss in their makeup.

Many characteristics define us as individuals, and there are many similarities between us.

Definite features in an emotional abuser seem to be much stronger than those same characteristics in the rest of us.

They have no empathy for anyone or anything, putting them into the realm of psychopaths and sociopaths which we'll discuss in the next chapter.

Is there something about your partner that seems to wear you down just by thinking about them?

When they walk through the door, everything very quickly becomes about them and what they want from you.

Many characteristics are common to all types of emotional abusers, but the one's highlighted below are the obvious ones I didn't take note of.

As they learn more about you, they expect to be rewarded for keeping them in check.

It is not so much about the secrets you may have, but more about what makes you tick.

The longer they keep you in the relationship, the more confident they are that they can demand anything from you without you arguing.

I received many threats over the years, and even though I was quite convinced that these threats were just hot air, I chose to err on the side of safety, which cost me dearly.

One thing about an emotional abuser is their uncanny ability to read a person.

About a week after meeting her, I asked her if she would like to join me for lunch.

She accepted, and we walked to a restaurant just down the road from where we were.

We sat at a table in the restaurant and got through the banalities of conversation quite quickly.

Then…

'Are you in a relationship?' she asked.

'Not at the moment.'

'Are you ready for one?'

'I suppose…'

These questions should have set off alarm bells in my head, but for some reason, they didn't.

How do you justify asking questions like these to someone you have never really had any form of meaningful conversation with?

You can't, unless you are asking these questions with a definite objective in mind.

It did not occur to me at the time that this exchange was her opening gambit in a mind game that was to last five years.

You need to understand that I was overweight and a socially awkward older bachelor who was being asked these questions by a slightly younger but beautiful woman.

As the relationship progressed, she got to know more about me and used this against me for many years. I was an open-book, but I had to drag personal information out of her.

I met her a few days after I had invested all my savings in a restaurant within the same group that I had been working at for ten years.

Now, when you do this, you look after your investment as closely as you can, and this was the first weak spot she picked up on within a few days of us meeting.

The easiest way she would get money out of me when we were apart was to threaten to come and see me at my place of business, as she knew I would not want her to make a scene.

She travelled the six hundred kilometres to my place of work on one occasion, just to make the point that I shouldn't doubt her when she said she would come and visit.

Always laying the blame on someone else

You will be blamed for all of the unhappiness your abuser experiences. Since the day I first met her, she has never accepted that anything that happened in her life was due to her behaviour. It was always someone else's fault.

It didn't matter to her that she was the one displaying the unacceptable behaviour. What justified her behaviour was her belief that she was entitled to behave in this manner due to previous wrongs she had experienced at the hands of others.

Through the years I heard many stories of how poorly she was treated by all those around her, and this is something that I can't dismiss offhand.

With her lying to me from the day we met, I was wary of anything she ever told me concerning her life before we met other than the drug abuse, as I experienced that first hand.

I understand that our formative years will be a driving factor into the person we become, but to keep on using this as an excuse to justify your behaviour within a relationship decades down the line, is not acceptable to me.

Unfortunately for me, I was made to pay for all of those wrongs.

Her mantra in life seemed to be 'Who can I blame for my problems; give me a second I'll think of someone.'

Narcissism is a distinctive feature

I believe that each emotional abuser must have a narcissistic side to their personality.

It may even be the most dominant part of their nature.

All emotional abusers will be incredibly charming at the start of your relationship.

They thrive on the fact that you are always on edge around them; they want you under their control at all times.

You are nothing to an abuser, except a source of supply of whatever they feel you have to offer them for being in a relationship.

They are with you not because they love you, but because you satisfy some crazy need that have within themselves.

The whole relationship has to revolve around them, and if it doesn't, they are going to manipulate you into making it so.

One thing you have to remember about a narcissist is that everything you ever say to them will be used against you while you are moulded into their bauble.

You may even hear from friends how lucky you are to have found someone so perfect. It is because they don't know who your partner is in the privacy of your home, and unfortunately you will never tell them either.

These are the three primary characteristics of my ex that I noticed during the entire time I was with her. I believe you can use these three as a rule of thumb to determine if your partner has the potential to be an emotional abuser.

I could probably list another fifteen or so characteristics, but the ones I gloss over below stand out above the others.

When you notice them in your partner, it should raise some serious flags as to the route your relationship is taking.

Extreme Jealousy is going to drive you nuts

I was never able to understand my partner's almost insane jealousy; it hung over our relationship every day.

Emotional abusers are an incredibly jealous group of people, and this is why they try and keep you and your behaviour under their control at all times.

We need to remember that jealousy is a sign of insecurity.

Their jealousy is something that is created in their mind, and unfortunately, you are going to bear the brunt of it.

It is not going to matter to the abuser how many times you try to convince them that the jealousy is unfounded. The minute they believe that you are 'unfaithful', you are going to hear all about it.

'Unfaithful' can be something as innocent as watching a TV show and an actress appears on screen:

'You think she's hot, don't you?'

'I'm just watching a TV show. Yes the woman is sexy, but so what. It's not like you don't find certain actors sexy, and I never question you about it.'

'We're not talking about me.'

It is here where a quiet evening in front of the TV turns into days of how I think every woman is more attractive than she is.

What is it about jealousy? Does your partner not realise that you are with them because you find them sexier than other women?

They are hypersensitive

Being hyper-sensitive is just a way of masking their deficiencies.

The most insignificant things you may say are going to be blown out of proportion.

Even the little things you used to joke about are suddenly going to become major issues. She will never forget anything you say to her during your relationship, and this WILL be used against you.

Everyone is out to get them.

They want you to believe that everything you do or say is to put them down and their responses are a form of protection against your perceived abuse of them.

The combination of her inability, or reluctance to control her behaviour, along with her hyper-sensitivity to everything, may have led to her emotional deficiencies.

Jumping to conclusions is another area where your abuser is going to drive you crazy. You are going to try and convince her continually that what she thinks is not the reality of what is happening in your relationship.

I guess that being hypersensitive could mean that you are more in touch with your own emotions than those around you and this may be the reason why emotional abusers have the gift-of-the-gab.

The other side of the coin is that they also tend to verbally attack the people who frustrate them rather than trying to work through an issue.

They tend to rush into relationships

I heard my ex tell friends and acquaintances that it was love at first sight.

It was more an issue of her rushing into a relationship because she didn't want to be alone or was she too lazy to look after herself.

This became evident the first day I took her out for lunch.

Had she just become used to having a man give her everything when and where she wanted and needed to continue the good life?

Whichever, I guess the 'love-at-first-sight' sounds more romantic to other people.

She believes that love is something that you can turn on and off at will with whoever you target.

As stupid as this sounds, it worked for me.

Using their gift-of-the-gab to confuse the heck out of you

We've all heard of or seen the good cop, bad cop routine in movies. These roles are played by two people in a room interrogating a third.

In an argument with an emotionally abusive partner, many more characters are thrown into this routine.

You'll have a good cop, bad cop, crazy cop, sane cop, child cop, adult cop and the list goes on.

The difference here is that all of these roles are played by the same person who is using their command of language and people behaviour to make sure they walk away from the argument as the winner.

Don't try and argue with your abuser. You have done it many times before without success, so what makes you think this time will be any different.

One thing you need to be clear of is that your abuser is arguing with themselves and you are a bystander listening to them rambling on.

They will ignore everything you say and will keep the argument going on in a circle for hours, if not days on end.

They are insincerely repentant

Apologies are something you are going to hear over and over again.

You'll hear them continually as your abuser has no intention of changing who they are, and how they behave.

They tell you what you want to hear, but there is no substance to what they are saying.

They are addicted to drama

They create drama and chaos around themselves and everyone they come into contact with.

Emotional abusers are a vicious group of people, and this tends to steer them toward the love they have for creating drama in your life.

The problems they create around themselves are more to draw you into their games than anything else.

You are going to try and solve the issue, but the more problems you solve, the longer you are going to find yourself stuck in your dysfunctional relationship.

Other behaviours to consider

In as much as they are trying to damage you emotionally, they are emotionally scarred going into a relationship.

The one moment they are going to be the person that you fell in love with, and the next, some crazy person who has lost the plot.

When in public, they can be charming and the perfect partner, but at home, a different persona is released on you that confuses you.

They are going to avoid talking about their feelings at all costs because they don't have any.

They will tell you it is too difficult for them to talk about their past. You can be sure of one thing though; if talking about their past benefits them in any way, they are going to share it with you at any given moment.

You will believe you are in a relationship with an adult child once you start counting the tantrums she throws over the years.

I can't remember how many times I asked her to 'grow up', but it never made a difference.

She is going to make sure that the stereotypical gender roles are played out in your relationship. You are going to have to provide everything material she needs, as well as for her well-being. If you don't do a good enough job, you will hear something along the lines of 'If you were a real man… or 'I wish you were like (put a friend's boyfriend or husbands name here).'

Be on the lookout for a drink and substance abuse issue before you move forward with your new relationship.

It is not to say that all emotional abusers have substance abuse problems, but if someone goes into a relationship like this, the possibility is much greater for these issues to be present.

She will have no respect for you or any interest in your feelings or opinions. You should pick up on this quite early in your relationship, but you will forgive her. I did, and it led to this book.

I believe that is an equation that female emotional abusers worm their way into your life.

Female emotional abusers are well aware that they are physically attracted to men, and it is this knowledge they use to make the initial contact. As men, the physical is the first thing we see, and it is this that piques our curiosity in someone new. We all want to say that this is not the case, it's her eyes, but come on.

Once you have seen that a physically attractive woman is showing interest in you, the woman knows she has you where she wants you.

We also want respect, approval and validation. It is the next set of variables that come into play, and this is where the real emotional connection takes place.

Once you have heard what you want to hear often enough, your partner turns herself into your daily fix.

You can't stay away from her. You want to be with her every single waking moment.

One of the leading variables at play here is patience.

She will take as long as it takes to achieve her goal of sucking you into her game.

It was a full month, to the day that I met her before there was any physical contact between us other than holding hands or a peck on the cheek.

That was when we had our first kiss.

Then the sex. Anytime. Anything. Anywhere.

Even though the sex was just the smallest variable in the equation, it sealed the deal for me. Having this incredibly beautiful woman wanting, actually insisting, to be my sexual partner was the best thing that happened to me.

Now that I was hooked, all hell broke loose in my life over the next five years.

An emotionally abusive relationship is designed by your abuser in the following sequence:

She puts her physical attributes front-and-centre in your daily life, adds a little approval, validation, respect and accomplishments, applies a tonne of patience to turn her into your daily fix and then throws the final ingredient, sex, into the mix.

This sequence of events happens naturally as any relationship develops, but an emotional abuser makes a conscious decision to use it in this exact sequence at specific times during the development of your relationship.

Nothing is left to chance.

Individual variables in the equation may differ when a male applies it to worm his way into a female victim's life, but the premise is the same.

Her behaviour during the initial stages of the relationship is an action that is there to be manipulated so that she eventually gets what she wants from you as well as from the relationship.

When added to the many other characteristics I will discuss in the following chapters, they make up a lethal cocktail that will eventually destroy your life if you allow it to do0 so.

3

BORDERLINE PERSONALITY DISORDER, BIPOLAR DISORDER, SOCIOPATH, PSYCHOPATH, OR NARCISSIST? WHICH ONE?

As much as we all love looking back to the day we met our partner for the first time and write it up to destiny: there is a simpler truth.

Many times we get drawn into a relationship because our future partner has made a quick assessment of our personality type and decided they can gain something from being in a relationship with us.

If you think about it, we are targets that turn into victims of emotional abuse.

I have still to come up with a better explanation of how I was conned into a relationship.

Cynical, yes; but oh, so true.

I have concluded that emotional abusers have a personality unique unto themselves as a group. It is an amalgamation of various types of personalities and personality disorders.

How can one person be negative, miserable, inconsiderate, financially irresponsible and entitled, manipulative, selfish, disrespectful and have no boundaries?

How can that same individual be prone to boredom, be a pathological liar, show no remorse or empathy, have no visible emotional range, accept no responsibility for their actions, have no long-term goals and strive on living a parasitic lifestyle?

That is why I maintain that an emotional abuser is a personality type on its own. There are many levels associated with the personality types I will gloss over. Put one or two traits of each type into a single person, and you have the perfect emotional abuser.

There are many personality types or disorders, that may be inclined to abuse someone emotionally, but I have selected the five below to create the ultimate emotional abuser.

- Borderline Personality Disorder
- Bipolar Disorder
- Sociopath
- Psychopath
- Narcissist

Each of these has their unique set of characteristics, but one common trait is the ability to flatter and turn on the charm. You are going to be flattered at every possible opportunity at the onset of your relationship. You are going to fall for it and love it at the same time.

It is especially the case if you are a thirty-nine year old, overweight, socially awkward bachelor who has a younger beautiful woman fawning all over you (me, in case you were wondering).

Your self-esteem is going to get such a huge boost that you may begin to wonder if you are the same person she is talking about.

Even though it makes you uncomfortable hearing someone talk about you in such glowing terms, you let it go on.

Okay, so maybe I had low self-esteem when I was sucked into the relationship; we'll get to that later.

What you need to be aware of is that this flattery is just the initial 'get your toes wet' on the part of your partner to see how far they can take it. Once you ask them to slow down a little with the flattery, the real person behind the facade takes a step forward.

What was once flattery when you were in a group and at home, just happens outside the walls of your home. Suddenly, at home you are worthless, but to everyone else you are still the perfect man.

In the meantime you are struggling to determine what brought about this change in your partner, which you don't even realise is who your partner is. You will eventually convince yourself that your partner is going through a bad time, even if this bad time lasts for years.

As men, we have been raised to believe that it is impossible for a woman to abuse a man in any form or manner, and as such, you begin to internalise everything you are going through. You won't even dare to speak to anyone about the situation for fear of being laughed at.

Sometimes I wonder if this type of abuser sees their relationships as more of a job than anything else.

As I mentioned in the introduction to this book, I am taking my understanding of these various personality types and disorders and not using clinical definitions to share my experiences.

Let's have a look at these types of personalities individually.

Borderline Personality Disorder

An inordinate fear of abandonment is a significant characteristic of those with Borderline Personality Disorder.

They become so dependent on you that nothing else seems to matter in their universe.

It appears they are also stuck in an emotional war zone where they are always struggling to understand how they are supposed to react with other people, in particular with those they are in close relationships with.

Their insecurities are projected onto others, and they emotionally abuse their partners even though they will in all likelihood, deny all knowledge of their behaviour.

They also use narcissistic behaviour as a defence mechanism and are master manipulators. They will attempt to keep you focussed on them at all times.

Their emotions are switched on and off at will, and they treat you with contempt all the while having a smile on their faces.

Everything you do for them will be misinterpreted as being selfish or having ulterior motives.

If you make them angry, they make you feel guilty; if you make them feel guilty, they will attempt to get you as angry as possible so that they can lay the blame at your feet for their behaviour.

You are either treated as a god or dirt; nothing in-between.

Their favourite tool of abuse has to be gaslighting; the means they use to convince you that your perception of being emotionally abused isn't correct.

They also seem to have a trait that makes them impulsive in many aspects of their life.

My ex went through money like there was no tomorrow, and most of it was spent on drugs and gambling.

I have lost count of the number of times she told me she was going to commit suicide.

About the third occasion, when we were still living together, she phoned me at work and informed me of her intention to commit suicide. She told me she intended to drink all her Bipolar medication to end her life.

My reaction was, I believe, quite typical. I rushed home to see if I could talk to her before she decided to go ahead with her plan.

Her reaction: wait to see me coming into the house, slam and lock the door as she sees me walking toward the bedroom, and proceed to swallow the pills.

I broke down the door and forcibly removed the remaining pills from her mouth. I didn't even think of taking her to the hospital.

That was the last time I rushed to her when she called me to say she was going to commit suicide. I eventually got to the point where I couldn't take this abuse any longer, and told her not to screw up and to get it right.

My response to her calls became: 'Yeah right; like I haven't heard that before.'

When I look back, it seems this tactic worked, as she hasn't threatened suicide for many years, and is still very much alive.

Something else that will become commonplace in your discussions is that the outcome of everything is always worst-case-scenario.

Her drug dealers were always demanding their money in 'an hour', or 'I am going to get beaten to a pulp; you'd like that wouldn't you?'

Don't think that any promise they make will mean anything to them. Write down the first broken promise made and just add to your list as your relationship moves along.

Bipolar Disorder

My understanding of Bipolar Disorder is that it isn't a personality disorder, it is more a case of being diagnosed with a clinical syndrome.

Even so, it wreaks havoc on a relationship.

I can only speak from my experiences of being in a relationship with someone who was diagnosed Bipolar I Disorder. I am by no means suggesting that everyone diagnosed with Bipolar Disorder is going to be emotionally abusive.

While in the relationship, I became convinced that she was mis-diagnosed, and it proved to be the case when she was diagnosed with Borderline Personality Disorder after ending up in a hospital with Stevens Johnson Syndrome[1].

That is an issue for the medical profession though.

There is this notion that when someone has a manic episode, they are not aware of what they are doing or saying at the time.

This is something that I never have, and never will subscribe to.

To witness, what I believed to be a manic episode, is an education in human behaviour. I can't believe that while in a manic episode you lose all sense of reality, do what you want to do and then plead innocence of all knowledge of what you had done or said. We must remember that a manic episode lasts for a period of time, be it a couple of hours or days. I am convinced that my ex was in a permanent manic state during the final year of our relationship.

I am more of the opinion that many a time, this destructive behaviour is justified by 'I didn't know; it must be my Bipolar Disorder, sorry.'

---

1   Stevens-Johnson syndrome, also called SJS is a rare but serious problem. Most often, it's a severe reaction to a medicine you've taken. It causes your skin to blister and peel off. It affects your mucus membranes, too. Blisters also form inside your body, making it hard to eat, swallow, even pee. www.webmd.com/skin-problems-and-treatments/stevens-johnson-syndrome#1

Every time my ex did something I didn't like, I told her. She was well aware of her behaviour at all times, whether she was manic or not.

Was her behaviour the result of a manic episode, or was the episode used as an excuse?

An excuse - I will never be convinced of otherwise.

Sociopaths

After we have been conned into a relationship with a sociopath, we fall under one of those evil spells from the fairy tales that we all heard about as kids.

We become oblivious to their behaviour through an irrational fear that they may leave us.

This fear ensures that everything you do is to please them. You must also not forget how they got into a relationship with you. Your ego and self-esteem were boosted to such an extent that you enjoyed the shaky pedestal you were put on.

Like narcissists and psychopaths, sociopaths will abuse you for as long as you allow them to. They are patient to the point of concentrating solely on you and what they can gain from you to the detriment of any other relationship they may be a part of.

There is only one sure outcome of getting into a relationship with a sociopath, and that is your destruction across all spheres; mental, physical and financial ruin awaits you.

You believe this the entire time you are in a relationship, but the reality is that you are being used to satisfy a need. If a sociopath displayed any feelings, the only one that would be evident, after the fact, is their hate for the person they are in a relationship with.

They will never put you above themselves with anything, but they will put you above all others as they are protecting an investment in their future.

Because of their charm and flexible personalities, sociopaths become the man or woman of your dreams.

They bear no moral responsibility towards society, and this dictates what they will do to achieve their goals.

Your relationship from the day you met was a ruse.

I often wonder when someone tricks you into a relationship if they feel as though they are loved.

Or do they know that this isn't the case and this is what forces them to behave in the manner in which they do?

This type of person has absolutely no boundaries, and consequences don't exist in the vocabulary of a sociopath.

They don't want the same as we do; love, respect and a sense of belonging to that something we call a relationship.

These emotions are below them.

Psychopaths

Psychopaths are master manipulators. They are capable of mimicking emotions without falling prey to them.

They have determined from the onset what your desires, fears, weaknesses and strengths are and will design a manipulation regime specifically for you.

Even though there may be a mutual attraction between you and your new psychopath partner, they trick you into believing that they truly love you. This loving nature of theirs continues until such a time that they see you are hooked on them, and the abuse will begin in earnest.

That 'loving' person you fell in love with will make the odd appearance just to make sure you stay interested in keeping them around, and ensuring that you get to the point where you believe everything you do is about keeping them happy.

Due to the covert nature of the manipulation and abuse, you never really understand what is happening until you break it off, if ever. Many years later, you still blame yourself for the disintegration of your relationship. Psychopaths get so deep into your psyche that you are unable to believe that they can ever do anything wrong.

They have no empathy and exploit people for a living.

My ex had an incredible sense of entitlement which may or may not have stemmed from her childhood. I was made to pay for every wrong that was ever done to her in the past, no matter what the source.

Her only motivation was to see how much money she could steal from me with the most incredible lies. She was self-centred, self-indulgent and wasteful. No matter how many times I spoke to her about this, nothing ever changed.

There was even a point in time when she tried to convince me that she had my child but the child was addicted to cocaine at birth, and I couldn't see my 'daughter' as she had been taken away by child services.

I think her ultimate goal was to see if she could annihilate me, and if that happened, only then would she possibly feel anything for me as I would have satisfied her ultimate goal.

One of the most frustrating things I had to deal with was her inability to learn from previous experiences. Poor judgement is inherent to her mindset. She was irresponsible, and you couldn't depend on her to do anything unless she benefited in some way.

I have to wonder if her excessive drug use had anything to do with the thrill-seeking nature of possibly being a psychopath.

I realise that not all people who display psychopathic characteristics turn violent, but I noticed a dangerous streak in my ex if her messages to me were anything to go by:

'I am going to kill you. Keep this message as proof that I want you dead. If I can't have you then nobody will. Your days are numbered. I have had enough of your snide remarks. Best we put them along with that pathetic mouth of yours where they belong - in the fucking ground. And this is not a threat; it's a promise. You insisted on kicking me while I was down, and laughed at me. Let's see who laughs last you ignorant piece of flesh. Poor excuse for a man. Come you want to fuck me up, when I get there and I will get there believe me. You can try all you need to stop me but you have now trampled on me enough"

'At least you don't have a problem expressing your feelings. Now all you have to learn is to tell the truth and you will be an amazing woman.'

'That was the absolute truth. It will give me great pleasure to put an end to your so called miserable life. You don't know what misery is. You think it's what you had the last four years. Think again. You will die a miserable death. We will die together. You are a fucking heartless, cold bastard and I will kill you. For every time u called me a whore, I will stab you once so you are going to look like a strainer when I am done with you.'

'Sleep well. Maybe you will feel better in the morning.'

'I won't sleep until I put you in the ground. You're a fucking asshole. U think u just get to break up with me. Not. If it ends, it will be with us both dead. Sorry to tell you but I have major rejection problems. Do u know what rejection can do to a person? Well you just did it to me. And believe you will pay dearly'

'Ok. Thanks for the warning.'

'Fuck off! You think this is a joke. I will kill you without hesitation.

That was not a warning, it was a preview. Hope you have very pleasant dreams. I love you to death'

As is quite evident in the above conversation between us, everything was my fault. She didn't believe that she had anything to do with the breakdown of our relationship.

Before you ask me about calling her a whore we need to put this into context.

At the start of the book, I mentioned that our relationship was mostly long distance.

I rented a house for us, but at this time my ex was at the height of her gambling and drug addiction. I was paging through a local publication, and a telephone number listed in an advertisement seemed to be very familiar. My ex had used nine telephone numbers up to that point to contact me. I went through the list, and the number that looked familiar was hers.

The major issue was that the advertisement was for her; she was advertising her services as an escort.

I confronted her about this and after the apparent initial denials, she admitted placing the advert and providing certain sexual favours for two men to get money for her drug and gambling addictions.

Of everything I had been through with her until that point, this was the one thing I could not forgive.

Narcissists

This personality type has an amazing ability to market themselves and are real proponents of the gift-of-the-gab.

Narcissists tend to hijack relationships. They will try and ensure that they occupy every single moment of your time.

We've all seen television shows or movies where police are interrogating a suspect in a tiny room. Living with a narcissist is almost the same as that. They will shut you out for periods of time and then carry on as though nothing is wrong. This creates immense confusion in your mind as to where you stand in your relationship.

They instil a fear that they may one day walk out on you; again, something you will attempt to avert at all costs.

A favourite tactic is they will make you feel guilty about something they have done. In your mind, it is almost as if you are the person who has committed a wrong.

This is a favourite when they are caught in a lie.

They will, from the onset, show an inordinate amount of affection to get the relationship moving forward quickly. This is especially confusing for someone who has never experienced this before.

These are your pathological liars as well as another group of master emotional manipulators.

They will take advantage of whoever can assist them in achieving their ends.

A narcissist doesn't have the capacity for empathy and therefore, has no feelings as to how their behaviour affects you.

Somehow, narcissists seem to draw you into a game where you almost without explanation, take on their emotions.

You empathise to such an extent that you forget about the reservations you may have about things that are going on in your relationship.

Once you have called them out on their behaviour and they can see you are on to their game plan, their behaviour suddenly becomes acceptable. This only lasts as long as it takes to suck you back into their confidence and they return to their normal behaviour of emotionally abusing you.

Narcissists create two personalities that they use to suck you into their game of emotional abuse. The first is the person you fell in love with; the loving, kind and understanding partner, and then the real narcissist; the person who has nothing but contempt for you and it has been this way for them all along.

As with all emotional abusers, the narcissist will never accept responsibility for their actions.

They don't care about anything.

You are going to tell them thousands of times to 'grow up.'

Don't be fooled for too long. This childish behaviour is being portrayed as it is helping them achieve whatever is on the agenda at that point.

One of the worst things we do as abused victims is give positive affirmation to our abusers when they are not abusing us.

We are always expecting the worst behaviour from our partners, but when the opposite happens, we see a sign of hope for the relationship.

The problem with this is that we then allow our abuser to continue with their behaviour toward us.

Each section of your abuser's personality is going to try and show you their 'softer' side, or reasons why they behave as they do.

As you become immune to the nuances of either the borderline personality disorder, bipolar disorder, sociopath, psychopath or narcissist, one of the others will kick in to take over the job of continuing the emotional abuse.

The old stories of how they were mistreated, abused or neglected as children will have shaped them into who they are, and will be shared with you at each apology they make for their behaviour.

Even though you are aware that their behaviour is to manipulate you, you are going to feel powerless to stand up for yourself.

As you have invested so much of yourself in the relationship, you feel that you need some return on your investment, and this is how these people get you to stick around for too long.

I can't speak to the manner in which the abuse may have manifested itself if there were children involved, but I am sure the kids would have been targets as well.

Remember, emotional abusers tend to focus on a single victim at a time, to help develop the 'he-said, she-said' defence for conversations with friends and family in the future.

They have created a social persona that everyone loves, and no-one is going to believe what you have to say about her behaviour.

4

EMOTIONAL ABUSE TACTICS.

There are many weapons in the arsenal of an emotional abuser that I can list, but the one that is most often used is fear.

The longer you live in fear, the more difficult it becomes to escape this type of relationship.

By fear, I am not talking about this relationship becoming physically violent, but more about the manner in which your thinking has changed through years of abuse. You have a constant fear that your partner may leave you as you have become so used to their behaviour you look at it as normal.

Your abuser will be of the mindset 'I will manipulate you into satisfying my needs, but if you want me to fulfil any of yours, I will point out how selfish you are.'

She used deceit, intimidation and any other means at her disposal to take control of our relationship.

We were about a year into the relationship when her true colours started showing. She never thanked me for anything unless I forced her to, and she had a massive sense of entitlement.

I can't even remember once where she showed me a little respect unless it was in her interest. She never loved me. She looked at me in the sense of how useful I would be in achieving her goals.

And boy, was I useful.

When you know that something is not right, tackle it head-on - don't leave it for another day. Don't hope that your partner made a mistake, and forgive her. This type of person does not make mistakes, everything they do is worked out to the finest detail.

You will continually be told that you don't care enough, or at all about your partner or any aspect of their lives.

They won't come straight out and say what they want; they will 'guilt' you into giving it to them.

Emotional deficiency must play a significant role in the lives of the emotional abuser. From the onset, you will notice that the only person putting any effort into your relationship is you. If your partner can't commit to your relationship or show emotion, the only way they will be able to keep you around is for them to abuse you emotionally into staying in the relationship.

An emotional abuser is neither interested in you nor loves you. Everything is about them and what they can get from you. You are nothing but supply to them.

If the following seems familiar, you are in all likelihood in one-half of an emotionally abusive relationship.

Demand

I want (*fill in the blank*) for…

Resistance

I know you are lying to me and you want the (*fill in the blank*) for something else.

Pressure and Threats

If I don't get (*fill in the blank*) then…

Compliance

Here's the (*fill in the blank*) because I don't want to be responsible for…

You can change this conversation to include anything that will be to the benefit of your abuser, but the outcome will always be the same. You will usually comply to keep the peace.

The more someone can manipulate you, the less they feel for you.

At the start of the relationship, you are seen as a challenge, but the longer you stay together, the less they care about you.

There are many things an emotional abuser will use to get what they want; things we wouldn't even consider:

Using your self-esteem against you

One of the greatest tools emotional abusers have is your self-esteem.

The object is to break you down so that you can be manipulated much more easily.

Our self-esteem is usually determined by mundane things such as weight, income and likeability.

These are the easiest areas to attack verbally; 'you are fat', 'you need to get an increase' and 'none of my friends like you.'

Yes, I heard these all and more.

A question I have asked myself many a time is:

Who suffers from lower self-esteem; the emotional abuser or the person being emotionally abused?

Does your abuser pile on the emotional abuse to make them feel better about themselves, or do you accept the abuse because you feel that you deserve it?

If your abuser has self-esteem issues, their behaviour will be destructive to themselves and those around them.

- Don't get into arguments with them; you will end up arguing for hours and not achieve anything.
- Don't try and 'fix' what you think may be wrong with them.
- Don't feel obliged to stay in the relationship

If you have self-esteem issues, I believe there is only one option open to you, and that is to talk to someone about what you are going through; be it with friends, family or a therapist.

Low self-esteem often leads you to behave in a manner which almost makes your thoughts turn into self-fulfilling prophecies.

Knowing that you have self-esteem issues, your abuser is going to use them to their advantage at every opportunity.

Take note how they will start finishing your sentences while you are having a discussion, and even during arguments.

They even speak on your behalf even though you have never said that they can do this.

My ex kept on telling people that I would be responsible for her debts, and I always came through for her.

Don't use external factors to determine your self-worth. You are more than just a physical being.

Guilt-mongering

The sympathy card falls squarely into this game.

They seem to be the only victims in the world. Everyone is always out to get them. Their previous lives were just about being on the receiving end of some injustice.

Your abuser has already determined that you have a problem saying no.

On one of many occasions that she will hear 'I will not be responsible for your actions any longer', she will know that you are feeling guilty about this before you have even finished speaking.

You have been conditioned by a guilt-monger to feel guilty if you say no.

Guilt-mongering is a tactic you need to be very aware of. You will have been conned into feeling an obligation that the responsibility of your abuser, actually belongs to you, and then they are going to guilt you into believing that this obligation is your responsibility.

You will have become accustomed to saying yes to your abuser and will be useless at setting boundaries.

The best remedy for this nonsense is to call their bluff. They are going to say that they didn't ask for your help.

Tell them 'OK, you will take care of it,' and walk away. Don't capitulate.

If you don't, you will have set no boundaries and your misery will be compounded for years to come.

Watch how quickly the story changes and how fast emotional manipulators can think as they come up with another story in real-time.

Gaslighting

Gaslighting is an old favourite of emotional abusers. They are masters at manipulating conversations and situations and turning them around to suit their own needs.

You are confident of what they have said, but they will put forward such persuasive arguments that you may begin to doubt your version of events.

What your abuser is trying to do with gaslighting is to keep you in a constant state of confusion to a point where you no longer trust your memory or judgment.

You will hear on a regular basis:

'I never said that.' You imagine things.'

'Why get upset over such an insignificant issue?'

'What are you talking about?'

Something I read recently, which I think is a brilliant idea, is to get a pen and a notebook and start taking notes when your conversations turn stupid.

Just tell your partner that your memory is failing and you need to take notes and refer her back to the questions she repeats continuously.

I can only imagine the reaction. I would have loved to have seen it.

Luckily we have emails and SMS's, and there is no denying where they come from.

I have been told on many occasions I have no proof that she sent those messages to me, even though the messages were sent from her email addresses or phone numbers.

She believes there is no way to prove anything, short of someone sitting next to her and confirming she presses enter after each message that she has ever sent to me.

Oh, and if there were someone to take a photo, that would be even better.

Mimicry

Mimicry is by far the easiest way an emotional abuser gets inside your head if you have a long-distance relationship.

How do you prove what you are being told?

You don't. You have to work on trust.

When your abuser eventually runs out of lies or forgets where they are in their current lie, then they need another way to manipulate you.

Mimicry is by far the most annoying way in which a person gets under your skin.

I can recall many incidents where she used events from my life to con me out of money for drugs and gambling, but two stand out.

I had mentioned that a brain tumour had caused my grandfather's death, and years later she used this to get money from me for a series of 'doctor's visits'.

What amazed me was the depth she went to researching treatment and medication for whatever ailment she supposedly had.

A few years into the relationship I told her that my youngest brother had been diagnosed with acute kidney failure.

Guess what. A week later, she complained of lower back pains and asked for money for another doctor's visit.

'I have acute kidney disease. I have to go for more tests and meds.'

'Amazing! A week after I tell you about my brother's kidney issues, you come down with the same thing. What stage?'

'Have no idea. You told me that your brother had kidney disease, nothing else. The doctor said that mine has probably got something to do with the abuse my kidneys have taken over the years with my drug use. This has got nothing to do with what you said about your brother.'

A few hours later I received a message:

'I have Hepatitis C. The doctor said that I need to go and see him as soon as I can.'

The first thing I did, was to research the causes and treatment for Hepatitis, not even questioning whether this was the truth or not.

Something told me a doctor won't tell you you have acute kidney disease, and a few hours later inform you the issue is with your liver, not your kidneys.

We had been going out for about eighteen months when the old jousting session of 'give me money' and my stock response at the time 'no', just became too much for me.

It was the final time I accepted any of her stories and I literally told her to f#$k off.

Over the years, I had sent her thousands of dollars for hospital visits, but when I broke it off with her, I received a series of messages from her within minutes which was possibly the first time she had ever told me the truth.

*'Every cent you gave me for the doctors over the past four years was not for that. The last time I was at the doctor was with my first pregnancy. All the money went for drugs and gambling. I was never raped. I never lost my passport. It was taken from me by a drug dealer. I used to run drugs between **** and ****. I never worked at ****. The money came from running drugs.'*

Those few sentences should you a clear indication of the tactics she used to keep me beholden to her.

Just to clarify, she did fall pregnant with my child during the first year we were together, but the pregnancy was ectopic and was terminated.

Your abuser uses mimicry because they are fully aware how you reacted to being in precisely the same type of situation previously and how it affected you. It is this premeditated behaviour that makes emotional abusers such an evil group of people.

They are counting on the fact that those same emotions you

experienced the first time are going to surface again which makes it much easier for them to get what they want.

Baiting

Baiting is another favourite once you have pointed out their behaviour to them. They do things in the hope of getting a reaction out of you, and you will invariably give them what they want.

I can remember one occasion where I was so tired of her behaviour that I slammed my hand down on the table in pure frustration.

You know, that frustration you experience when it feels you are all alone in the world and there is no one you can approach to take some of the burdens from you.

Well, she said I had a hidden violent streak, and she was afraid I would use it against her. During many arguments after I hit the table top and found ourselves in a heated argument, she would say 'do you feel like hitting me? Why don't you do it then?'

This tactic will be used by your narcissist abuser.

Baiting validates the existence of your abuser. They need to get a reaction from you to ensure that their tactics have the desired effect on you.

Baiting is used mostly to get emotional reactions out of you.

You may get a message along the lines of:

'I am sorry I caused you so many problems. I am going to do something extremely drastic today, and I just want to say I am sorry.'

I had received hundreds of similar messages from her over the years, yet I still wanted to know what her radical plan was.

I knew it wouldn't be suicide or anything that would cause her physical harm. It would be something that I had been hoping to hear for many years, but I had to know.

'What are you going to do?'
'Don't worry about it.'
'Ok.'
'You don't care what happens to me, do you?'
'You don't want to tell me, what am I supposed to say.'

Then silence. The messages stop for an hour or two and every message you send to find out what is going on is ignored.

Then beep beep.

'I am going to the hospital to see if I can get an appointment with a psychologist at Mental Health. I realised last night how far I am gone. I need help. Urgently!'
'Yeah, right.'
'Wayne, I didn't sleep last night thinking about how I have treated you over the past few years, and I want to change. I love you. I need to ask if you can send me $50 to go and see the doctor and for medication I may need afterwards.'
'Why don't you just ask for money instead of lying to me? We both know you are going nowhere near a hospital voluntarily.'
'Please Wayne. I need help! I am going to the doctor. I was there earlier today to find out what a consultation would cost.'

Against my better judgment, I sent her the money, and guess what; she never went to a hospital, and still hasn't to this day.

One thing I learned over the years was that it worked against me to ignore this type of message from her.

I could ignore her messages for a day, but longer than that, and it started to get ugly, even from my side.

She would start threatening my life and my business.

I started using words and phrases I thought I would never say to another human being, and this scared me.

By the time the whole argument is over, you automatically forgive her thinking that your language provoked her reaction when in reality, the opposite was true.

Baiting changes how you would typically respond to a given situation.

Where you would usually think before acting, baiting takes this reasoning away from you.

Your reactions move from being reasonable and calculated to base and reactionary; you want relief from the situation right now.

In my case, it was the language I used. I would throw every insult I could come up with at her, even though I knew this wasn't who I was.

Don't get into an argument with someone who is baiting you; this is exactly what they want.

Something else to consider with baiting is the old 'bait and switch' tactic - a subtle form of blackmail.

In the initial stages of your relationship, you are going to be the hero, the perfect partner and she will jump in to take your side whenever she feels you may be losing an argument.

She has learnt all your opinions, thoughts and ideas on every subject you have ever discussed. She will ask your opinion on something and knowing what you are going to say, will knock down any opinion you may offer.

I can list many more tactics that get used to keep you confused, but the ones listed below are used most often.

I haven't gone into them in any detail as they all make up a part of the other tactics mentioned earlier in the chapter.

Blame Shifting

Whatever the issue, it is always someone else's fault.

By continually blaming others for who she was, my ex had decided there was no need to change her behaviour.

It was always something *made me do it*, instead of admitting that she was well aware of the choice she was making.

She tried to convince me there was no alternative way to react to a given situation at the time.

The brilliance of this tactic is that many times it is so subtle you don't even realise that she shifted the blame to someone or something else.

As a master manipulator she will throw some contributing factors into her explanation that at the time, you will consider being reasonable.

In your mind, this quickly diminishes the role she played in this situation.

You need to hold your partner accountable for their actions, but this is easier said than done.

Projecting

There are two sides to this tactic.

Firstly, it masks your partner's feelings, be they blatant or repressed and secondly, your partner blames you for what you are accusing her of.

I heard many a time that I was thinking of leaving her, but this was down to her Borderline Personality.

Her extreme jealousy led her to accuse me of looking for someone else, but maybe this is what she wanted; someone else.

Many years after we separated, I still received the odd telephone call from her.

When I say odd, I mean that her record number of telephone calls to me in an evening was 157.

Thankfully her number is blocked on my phone, so I don't know about the calls until I see my missed call log in the morning.

It irritated me to the point of exploding, and the result of this was to call and ask why so many calls?

Her immediate response to answering the phone would be along the lines of 'What do you want?'

She was irritated with me for calling her once in response to 157 phone calls from her.

I tried my butt off to make our home as normal as I could and provide whatever she needed. When something didn't go her way, then it was 'you don't care for me like you used to.'

I learned through many years of frustrating conversations that all she was doing was telling me that she has no feelings for anyone, or she had done something she didn't have the courage to judge herself over and chose to attack me rather than accept responsibility.

Shifting the goalposts

She changes the issues being discussed to avoid answering something. You never know where you stand.

This is where her manipulation tactics came to the fore.

Once you confront her about something, she starts talking in circles, and you are going to get lost in the confusion of it all, or you are going to do something that she doesn't like, and in response, something that you enjoyed from her side is going to disappear.

I love reading, and my ex and I always used to read for a few minutes in bed before going to sleep at night.

She once gave me a book to read from an author she enjoyed, but I didn't, and I told her so.

The very next night, and from that point forward, when I opened my book, she just rolled over in bed and switched off the bedside lamp on her side of the bed.

I left it for a few days and then asked her why she doesn't read in the evening any longer.

Her response was: '*It's obvious you don't appreciate me bringing you anything so I don't see the point.*'

In a fraction of a second, she wiped out a nightly ritual we had created over a few months without even blinking an eye.

I have mentioned that manipulators never forget anything you say, do or have told them, and this is where that comes into play.

Evasion and diversion come to mind.

Minimising

'It's not that bad.'
'I can't believe you thought that I was serious.'

These are often used in conjunction with denial.

'I didn't say that. I would never say something like that.'

This tactic is used by someone who is out to convince you that whatever they did wasn't as bad as they know it was or as bad as you think.

They will often accept responsibility for a small part of the issue, but not the worst part.

We can add blame shifting as a cousin of minimising.

None of these tactics are used individually to draw and keep you in an emotionally abusive relationship.

Seen in isolation and out of context, they may seem quite manageable.

It is a combination of tactics that make it so difficult for you to realise you are emotionally abused.

5

CODEPENDENCY

The most accurate definition I have seen regarding wording for co-dependency is:

'Excessive emotional or psychological reliance on a partner, typically one with an illness or addiction which requires support.'

Ouch…

I couldn't have described myself better if I had written the definition.

Co-dependency is as much a tactic of emotional abusers as it is a state that you as a victim will find yourself in. It warrants its own chapter as this is the worst thing that can happen to you within your relationship.

Of all the mistakes I made, and we'll get to those in the next chapter, co-dependency was the worst trap I fell into.

The quickest way to determine if you have a co-dependent personality is to ask yourself if the welfare of others crosses your mind before your own well-being.

If this is the case, this very moment is the time to take stock of what you are feeling about the manner in which your relationship is progressing.

Look out for the signals and stop them as soon as they become apparent to you.

Here are a few things you may recognise in yourself that may indicate that you are on your way to becoming codependent on someone.

- You don't have any friends of your own.
- You worry about what your partner would do if you decide to leave.
- You want to spend as much time as you can with your partner, to the detriment of any other relationships you may be a part of.
- You wait to see what mood your partner is in before you make any decisions or say anything.
- You become so used to being the giver in your relationship that you begin to wonder why you get nothing in return.
- You're trying to 'fix' someone.

There will be some form of co-dependency within any relationship, but when your partner seems to be the only thing on your mind, you may be co-dependent.

My partner was co-dependent on me for money for drugs and gambling, as well as a roof over her head.

She had used all of the tactics highlighted in the previous chapter to make me co-dependent on her.

I helped dig the hole I was in within my relationship, and she just kept on piling sand on top of me. I had this inherent need always to solve the problems my girlfriend created; be it gambling, drug debts, or lies she had gotten so deep into that I believed she could not solve. Most of the time, these were just blatant lies on her part to con me out of money, but even though I knew deep down that I was being lied to, I always wanted to give her the benefit of the doubt.

I had this strange notion that one day she would return to being the person I fell in love with. Don't waste your time trying to change the behaviour of an emotional abuser. I firmly believe I was that one person who was picked out from a crowd whom she believed had a co-dependent personality and manipulated me into a relationship. It is as though there is a form of duality at work here, truth/lies and emotional abuser/co-dependent.

I was unable to say 'No' to her.

How stupid does one have to be to continually give someone a chance, when you know full well they will never change and are just using you? This is where co-dependency is so dangerous; you may eventually make decisions that in normal circumstances you would never make. You may even be drawn into becoming an unwilling co-conspirator in the chaos that your partner is creating around your lives.

Your self-worth and self-esteem are so low that you want to please everyone all the time.

You have an idea of how things should be, and this becomes the driving force in your relationship.

You become a fixer, and your life and emotions get put on hold as you try and make sure that everything your partner wants or needs given to her, regardless of the personal consequences.

You firmly believe it is your responsibility to fix any issue your partner may have created.

The boundaries between your needs and those of your partner become so blurred that you can't differentiate between the two.

Even though you feel responsible for your partner's behaviour, on some level, you hold her responsible for yours. You will blame her for 'forcing' you to do things to please her even though they go against your better judgment.

The toll my enabling behaviour had on my mental state was debilitating. Every minute I was apart from my girlfriend, I was always wondering what nonsense she was getting into, and what I was going to have to do to help her out of it.

One of the worst things that co-dependency does to you as a person is it takes you out of the game. Your personality, your talents and desires are put on hold so that you can 'look after' your partner. You are not you any longer. It creeps into other aspects of your life. In my case, I was too afraid to ask my boss for a raise for almost three years, even though I was working fifteen hour days for months on end without a day off. You withdraw into your shell, and anything, within reason, anyone does to you is acceptable. Everything that happens to you is meant to be.

The biggest issue I had was my partner being a cocaine addict and leaving drug debts all over the place.

As we were living apart, and me being aware of the drug addiction, I never questioned her when she called me to say there was a drug dealer after her and she needed to pay up 'now'.

I was worried about what would happen to her if the drug debt wasn't paid, and she knew this and played on this for a long time.

Even though I came to realise she was using me to buy drugs, for some reason, I couldn't seem to stop myself from giving her money.

I was willing to make too many personal sacrifices to prove my love for my partner.

It was as though I was living to support my girlfriend's addictions.

You are going to excuse your partners selfish and narcissistic behaviours continually.

One of the things that co-dependency builds in you over time is a feeling of resentment toward your partner.

You do everything you believe your partner needs but are left feeling unappreciated. Even though you feel unappreciated and used, you still don't want to avoid your primary duty of satisfying whatever need your partner may have.

You walk around in a constant state of anger, even though you may not express this. You are angry at your partner for making you behave as you do, but you also don't want to do anything about it.

A side-effect of my co-dependency is that I developed my own addiction to separate my mind from what was happening in my relationship on a daily basis. Luckily I did not turn to drugs or gambling, but I have come to realise that I turned to food. I have always been overweight, but I put on 26kg during the time we were together, and ballooned to 148kg.

By the time this book is published, I will be well on my way to losing this weight. Firstly I had to get rid of the reason for the weight, and now I can get rid of the weight.

Writing these words made me realise I too suffer from a personality disorder: co-dependent personality disorder.

Not sure if this exists, but if it doesn't, it should, and I would sign up for whatever therapy or help that may be deemed necessary to get myself sorted out.

Emotional abuse and co-dependency in a relationship feed off each other in such a manner that is damaging to any relationship.

Loving someone doesn't mean that you have to give everything you have to the point of destroying yourself.

Stop thinking about your partner 100% of the time; yes that is a good thing.

The best way to start breaking your co-dependency is learning to say no without explaining yourself to your abuser.

One of the quickest ways to jolt yourself back to reality is to ask yourself a few questions:

'What do I want from this relationship?'
'What would make ME happy?'
'What are MY likes or dislikes about this relationship?'

Your behaviour of satisfying every need of your partner over a period of time is going to make it very difficult to start thinking about yourself first, but YOU HAVE TO.

Your partner may not like the new you and will see her control diminishing. She may threaten or decide to leave.

If this is the case, it is her choice: help her pack and close the door behind her as she leaves.

I have come to realise that for any relationship to flourish, both partners need a little 'me' time. Give each other room to breathe.

If you are responsible for the happiness of your partner, then who is responsible for yours? Not your partner; all she wants to do is control you.

With the two of us being co-dependent, there was a struggle to see who was going to have the greatest authority in the relationship.

I was trying to 'fix' what I thought was wrong with my girlfriend, and she was seeing if she could get me deeper into her game of deceit.

Einstein's definition of insanity comes to mind; doing the same thing over and over and expecting different results.

Having read this far into the book, you know that she won that battle hands-down, but now that I am single, I think about how my stupidity took me on a journey through emotional hell.

6

MISTAKES THAT ALL VICTIMS OF EMOTIONAL ABUSE MAKE

Even though we are victims of our partners, our stupidity allows us to be emotionally abused for much longer than is necessary. If we just thought logically at the onset of the relationship, we would never repeat the same mistakes continuously.

It eventually gets to the point where you have to ask yourself:

'What the heck am I still doing here? I've been through all of this before, so there must be a pattern to her behaviour that is never going to change. With that being the case, do I still want to be here?'

We remain the 'nice guy' for too long in the relationship, and this is what leads us to suffer at the hands of our abusers for longer than necessary.

We believe that we are involved in a relationship; it isn't a relationship, it's an entanglement.

There are just too many emotional factors missing to call what you are experiencing a real relationship.

There are many mistakes we make, but the ones I'll go through here are those that kept me in my relationship for far too long.

Believing that I was at fault

There are many tactics these abusers use to worm their way into your life.

The end game here is that they want you to believe you are to blame for their behaviour at all times. It becomes so because they say so often enough and you start to believe it.

The quicker you come to realise that you are not to blame for the situation, the faster you will build the confidence to walk away.

The major factor contributing to you accepting the responsibility for your situation is the continual state of denial you live in.

Am I misunderstanding her?

She must have heard and understood what she just said to me.

Someone who says she loves me couldn't have done that.

I can go on and on.

When you have been in a relationship for an extended period, you come to know your partner and can predict with a great level of certainty how they are going to respond given a particular set of circumstances.

Below is an exact quote, copied and pasted from one of her emails to me, that explains exactly how a master manipulator thinks.

'I am sorry I have lied to you so much and I lie to you most of the time because you tell me what to lie about. Every time you tell me that I am going to do something I do it because if you are going to be mad at me, then let it be for a valid reason.'

When I read these two sentences for the first time, I thought that I didn't understand what she had written.

I re-read them to come to grips with what she was saying; it was my fault that she was lying to me.

It is also tacit proof that she intended was to keep me in a constant state of confusion so that I would either not concentrate on, or forgive her behaviour.

Continually forgiving her behaviour

Never forgive or minimise an abuser's behaviour as that is what they are counting on you to do over and over again to draw you deeper into the cycle of abuse.

The longer you allow it, the longer it is going to carry on.

You will forgive your abuser the first time they apologise as you have yet to discover that you are in an emotionally abusive relationship.

Forgive the same behaviour a second time, and already you should be asking yourself a few questions about your partner.

Forgive for the third time, and you are going to find it very difficult to walk away from your abuser.

Every subsequent occasion you forgive your partner just makes it easier for them to continue with the abuse.

By now, you have been convinced by your partner that they are not to blame for their behaviour. You may even believe that you are the cause of some of this behaviour.

Trying over and over shows your abuser how deeply they have sucked you in, and you are permitting them to continue with their routine.

Don't ever allow yourself to justify their behaviour; there is nothing that can justify this sort of conduct.

Stop it!

The easiest way to perpetuate the forgiveness cycle is by not setting boundaries on their behaviour, and even if you do, you don't stick to them.

These limits must have a set of consequences attached to them, which have to be non-negotiable.

Don't ever budge on the consequences. The first time you do, it is game over for you.

Forgiveness is seen as weakness, and it will be taken advantage of.

Confront them directly over their behaviour, stick to the consequences, and you may have built yourself a little deterrent for a behaviour of this type in the future.

The only real consequence should be that you walk away as quickly as you can.

Feeling a sense of responsibility for her behaviour

My ex got me to the point where I felt responsible for her actions.

The longer I felt guilty, the more decisions I made that were entirely out of character.

By doing this, you are ensuring that you will never see who your partner is. Remember that emotional abusers don't get into relationships; they target their next victim. They are all too willing to put on a show for however long it takes to remove you from seeing the worst in your partner.

I didn't know going into the relationship that the reason she was new in town was that she was running away from drug debts in her hometown.

Her family, whom I saw on a regular basis at our restaurant before I even met her, also forgot to mention this.

After the initial month or so of dates, she started coming over to my house to stay over for a night, especially on a Friday. Then she would stay the whole weekend, and before I knew it, she had moved in with me.

I knew this was her intention all along, as she was working and living about twenty kilometres from the centre of town, and it was very challenging, time and transport wise, for her to get to and from work in the mornings. She was living with her aunt and uncle at the time.

We set up home, and initially, all went well. She went to work every day, got back just after six in the evening, which suited me fine, as I would race home to her at about seven. We got into the whole domestic routine of cooking together, washing dishes together, and sitting on the sofa to watch a little television or a movie in the evenings. We would then cuddle up in bed and fall asleep in each other's arms. Bliss, yeah right! The old saying 'if things seem too good to be true, they probably are', springs to mind.

Within weeks of moving in with me, she suddenly lost her job. I asked why, and the response to this, and to her losing subsequent jobs, was that no-one wanted to offer her a permanent position after her initial probationary period of three months. This seemed very strange to me, as she is a smart and intelligent woman, but I was in love and did not question anything she told me. A huge mistake. In a relationship, you need to question everything that does not make sense from day one, or else you will be used as a doormat for the duration of your relationship. Each time I asked her to give me a contact number of someone at her work, there was always an answer; 'you will make me look foolish' or 'they don't want to talk to you because they are employing me and not you', or numerous variations on these.

Life was good for a few weeks, and then I started noticing that money was disappearing from my bank account. I did not check my bank statements on a regular basis, as I was the only person who had access to my accounts. Initially, I thought I had forgotten about some withdrawals because I was under the impression that I alone knew what my PIN code was, as well as for the fact that I mostly kept my banking cards locked up in my safe at home when I was at work. If I needed money urgently, my home was five hundred meters away.

Money was going missing on a weekly basis, and eventually, the amounts became larger and larger. Two weeks later, I contacted my bank and asked them to look into how this money was going missing when I knew for certain that I was not making the withdrawals. It did not even cross my mind that someone very close to home was the ATM thief. It had taken about three weeks before a definitive answer was given to me by the bank. My new girlfriend was taking the money from my account. I confronted her about this, and initially, the obvious denials were forthcoming. It was when I took her to the bank and walked into the security office asking if they would show me footage from the ATM outside the bank, did she admit to taking the money. She admitted this before the security personnel at the bank even responded to my request.

We got home, and I asked her why she was doing this when all she had to do was ask for money if she needed it - no response. I then asked her how she had managed to get my PIN number. Silence.

I suddenly realised that every time I went to the ATM to withdraw money, she insisted on going for a 'walk' with me. Also, when I inserted my card into the ATM, she would be standing right next to me. It did not even cross my mind that she was memorising my PIN number those times we went to the bank together. I was in love. I had locked her passport in my safe at the house and had given her the combination in case she needed her passport for anything. She had seen my bank cards and had hatched a plan to get access to them, knowing full well that I rarely withdrew money from the cards due to the high banking fees charged when you use your cards in a foreign country. More money went missing from my account a few days later, and my ex denied that it was her. I threatened to lay a charge of theft against her at the police, and only then did she admit to stealing from me again.

In the meantime, she had ensured that I had fallen hopelessly in love with her. To this day I regret not telling her to leave when she did not stop stealing from me, but what is a thirty-nine-year old, overweight bachelor supposed to do. Your heart tells you not to let her go. What are the odds that you will find someone to share your life with at that age? She knew that I would forgive her, and she could already see that I was going to be very easy to control as long as we were together.

Eventually, I asked her what she was doing with the money, and then the 'truth' came out. She told me that she was a gambling addict, and would go to the casino at any opportunity she could. When I eventually stopped her from taking money, certain things of high value disappeared from my house.

It is a testament to her planning that nothing ever went missing when it was just the two of us in the house. When someone came and did some work, or delivered something to the apartment, my property would go missing. I was at work during the day, and as she was at home, she would attend to all of those people who came to the house. I would only notice things missing a week or two after these people were at the house.

First, it was the iPod my family gave me for my birthday, and then the accessories went missing a short while later. Then it was little things like pens and external hard drives. She was selling anything of mine she could lay her hands on. When there was nothing left to sell, she went to my friends and asked them to lend her money on the premise that she would pay them back once she started working. She asked them not to say anything to me. I still can't, to this day, figure out why no-one came to me and told me about her borrowing money from them.

Eventually, she did find employment, and she seemed happy in the initial stages to fall into the routine that so many of us find ourselves in. Wake up, have coffee, go to work, have lunch, work some more, go home, help cook dinner, watch a bit of television, and then go to bed.

A narcissist tends to get bored very quickly, and eventually she lost her job. I did not know this, as she would leave the house at the same time each day and return just after five in the afternoon.

She was gambling during the day with money she had borrowed or saved. Our friends had seen her on numerous occasions at the casino during the day. She had even approached some of them asking them not to tell me that they had seen her there. They never did tell me.

I was amazed that each time she returned from the casino, she had never lost any money. She always broke even or walked out with a little extra. We all know that the odds are stacked in favour of the house winning, but she seemed to be beating the odds.

I never laid eyes on a single cent she had supposedly won. One of the worst things she did after she lost her job to get money for gambling, was to steal a car. One of her ex-colleagues made mention of the fact that he needed to buy a vehicle, and she offered to help him source a car within his price range. Within days, she told him she had found a vehicle, but he had to pay her cash up front so that she could make the transfer to the seller and have the documentation for the sale sorted out.

Without question, he handed over the $ 3,500.00. By this time, she had already accepted a job a few hundred kilometres away and was already packed to leave. The money she received for the 'sale of the car' was used to feed her gambling habit. She then left for her new job.

I only found out about this 'transaction' a month later when a mutual friend of ours said something in passing. I was floored by what I heard. I immediately offered to return his money, which I did a few days later. He just forgave her, citing that he knew about her gambling addiction from the day she arrived on the scene. Returning the money was my step into the abyss.

My ex immediately took this as an indication that whatever debt she made, I would pay off for her. My stupidity led me to do exactly that.

It is impossible to ask a gambling addict to stay away from the casino. Eventually, I forced her to go to the local gaming authorities and ban herself from the casino for one year.

Even though she had banned herself from the casino, an addict on a mission, be it obtaining drugs or finding a casino to gamble at, is impossible to stop.

Once she had moved away to start her new job, she began gambling almost immediately.

She told me only the good things about her past and conveniently forgot to mention all the baggage she brought into our relationship.

By the time all of this came out, we were already a year into the relationship, and I had already been moulded into the toy she needed to give her whatever she was looking for at the initial stages of our relationship.

Using her behaviour against her

For those of you involved with an emotional abuser over a period of time, it is tough not to take on some of their behaviour as a defence mechanism.

It is perfectly normal that you will reach a level of frustration with your partner's behaviour and that your anger will boil over.

You will start using the same tactics you are experiencing in the hope that they can see 'what it feels like'.

You are going to say things that, after the fact, you won't believe came out of your mouth.

Unfortunately, because of who you are, you are going to feel an immediate sense of guilt for what has just happened.

The knee-jerk result is to forgive her for making you so angry, but it is not the correct response.

All this does is give your abuser more ammunition for the future and will rarely achieve the desired effect of getting your partner to change their behaviour.

I lost my temper on many occasions, used inappropriate language, made threats to kick her out, and if I look back, I realise that I apologised for my behaviour.

She never did, not once.

Living in a fantasy world instead of embracing reality

We all have that optimistic streak within us, but there comes a time when we need to face reality.

As much as we force ourselves to believe that our partner is going to change, after a year or two of their repetitive abusive behaviour, it is time to wake up.

Forgiveness and accepting responsibility for their behaviour play a part in creating this illusion in your mind of a partner who is having a bad day, even if this bad day goes on for years.

As difficult as it is to face and accept what is happening in our relationship, it is something we have to do for our sanity.

Realising that you are an actor in a horror story and not some fairy-tale, may help change your outlook on the situation.

Not even the witches in those fairy-tales have anything on my ex to her propensity for evil.

The worst part of this 'fantasy world' of ours is that it is self-created, as we are always covering up our partner's behaviour to those outside our home.

This just tells your abuser that their behaviour is acceptable, as you will never tell anyone the truth of what you are experiencing.

A consequence of our mistakes is we feel that we deserve whatever emotional pain we experience during our relationships.

7

WHY I FELL FOR MY ABUSER

Other than making the mistakes I mentioned in the previous chapter, many other personal issues put a sign on my back stating that I was ready to be emotionally abused.

I didn't walk into the relationship knowing that I was going to be emotionally abused. In fact, I had no idea that this form of abuse existed. I had heard and read about verbal and physical abuse, but never emotional.

I mean, how could someone dig so deep into my being and abuse me emotionally?

In the initial stages of the relationship, I wasn't even aware that I was being abused. I thought the endless arguments we were having were just a regular part of a developing relationship. It didn't occur to me that we were arguing about the same thing all the time; her behaviour and actions that didn't make sense to me.

Much of what I have read, states that people put up with emotional abuse because they have become accustomed to a level of comfort that they have developed within their relationships. They don't have to make decisions and worry about financial or other issues within the relationship.

I was different. I was the one making money and making the decisions in my life, yet I let someone in who turned everything upside down.

I was aware of how I was being treated and had this crazy notion that my abuser would eventually change if I helped her realise how she was hurting me.

Why?

If I had to point out the single primary cause leading to my emotional abuse, it would be that I had no idea as to the workings of a healthy relationship with a woman.

I have always been incredibly shy of women, and the fact that I had self-esteem issues with my weight, forced me to become comfortable with my own company and a good book.

The downside of this is that you tend to believe you are the only person who can solve your problems. You keep everything internalised, and you never look for guidance from anyone.

Even my date for my High School dance was arranged by my best friend as I was hesitant to ask the girls in my class.

Looking back, I realised I didn't go on a single date the whole time I was in High School.

Even at my age, I was very naïve when it came to the workings of relationships.

Another contributing factor has always been that I am too patient for my own good and could not say 'No'.

In turn, this led me to believe that I was responsible for all the chaos in my relationship, even though I had nothing to do with creating it.

I was stuck with being who I was and having a beautiful woman courting me led me into a relationship with blinkers on my eyes.

I was stuck with someone who was taking care of my basic emotional and physical needs, no matter how brutal the experiences were.

What I thought was the standard progression of a relationship, was a recurring cycle of abuse.

I still ask myself why I fell for my abuser and ignorance and stupidity are the recurring answers.

You are not stupid by being drawn into this. Nobody is prepared for how manipulative an emotional abuser can be.

You just have certain vulnerabilities that allow you to be sucked into this type of relationship.

You are going to feel stupid after-the-fact once you realise that all the signs showed your relationship wasn't a normal one.

I'm now at that point in my life that if someone expresses interest in becoming involved in a relationship, there is going to be a questionnaire to fill out:

1. Why are you single?
2. Why are you interested in me?
3. Why did you break up with your previous partner?
4. Are you, or have you been, a drug or gambling addict?
5. Are you honest about your motives for going into a relationship?
6. Are you trustworthy?
7. How will you get what you want from me?

I can probably come up with a hundred questions about your favourite colour and what TV programmes you like, but those don't tell me anything about who you are.

Sorry about the 'job-interview' type questions, but my emotional abuser looked at me as a long-term project, rather than a relationship.

I know I can, and should, live without my abuser, but HOW?

She is still such a part of my thought processes, and I doubt if that will ever change, but I sincerely hope it will.

I had such a deep connection with her that she became my first and last thought, and everything in-between, each day.

Now, I would rather be alone, than have someone around me acting as though they have feelings for me.

I would rather be alone than have someone use me as a toy in the game they call a relationship.

I listened to my heart, and not my head, and this allowed me to be drawn into a relationship with an emotional abuser.

Something else I thought about at length is - what if I was addicted to pain; not physical, but emotional pain.

This is also the primary reason why I made excuses for my ex's behaviour for such a long time.

My naivety, going into this relationship may have disguised my lack of emotional preparedness for any form of adult relationship.

To all of those judgmental people out there who blame you for being a victim of emotional abuse; you are as naive as I was going into my relationship.

I am still hurting, and to get me to commit to a relationship again is going to take one exceptional lady, who has no problem completing my questionnaire.

8

REASONS FOR WALKING AWAY.

1. I am tired of your incessant lies.
2. I am limp of constantly catching you out in your lies.
3. I am worn of you saying that you lie to me because you don't want to lose me.
4. I am exhausted of waiting for things to change.
5. I am sick of your hollow promises of change.
6. I am weakened of you continually saying that you are sorry.
7. I've had enough of your crocodile tears.
8. I am disabled by not being in a loving relationship.
9. I am drained by being used by you.
10. I am frazzled by you always playing the victim.
11. I am annoyed at your laziness.
12. I am unnerved by the number of times you have told me you are starting a new job, and nothing happens.
13. I am weary of your selfishness.
14. I am tired of not being respected by you.

15. I am sick of being your meal ticket.

16. I am irked by your threats.

17. I am crippled by our constant arguing.

18. I am enervated by the fact that we don't laugh together anymore.

19. I am fatigued by not feeling appreciated.

20. I am drained by you manipulating me.

21. I am devitalised by your lack of emotion.

22. I am distressed by you never listening to what I have to say.

23. I am blown by your impulsiveness.

24. I am exasperated by your lack of ambition.

25. I am unnerved by being the only one making sacrifices.

26. I am sick of always thinking that I must get out of this relationship.

27. I am impaired by the feeling that our relationship has been a sham.

28. I am irritated by you using my love for you as a means to get what you want.

29. I am constricted by always worrying about what you get up to when we are apart.

30. I am nauseated by you continually blaming your past for your problems.

31. I have had enough of being the one made to pay for all the wrongs done to you in the past.

32. I am debilitated by feeling that the one thing remaining for you is to annihilate me.

I can go on and on, but I think we all get the idea of how you are going to be treated by an emotional abuser.

9

THE UNSENT LETTER.

Dear ......,

I do still love you, and there will always be that little corner of my heart reserved just for you, even though you destroyed me both emotionally and financially.

I have loved you from the day we met and through all that has come and gone, but the time has come that I walk away as I am unable to cope with your constant lies and the emotional abuse I have suffered at your hands during the past five years.

I won't sit around any longer and hope that you are going to change; there is nothing more important to you than cocaine, heroin, gambling and lying, and there never will be.

I cannot compete with the highs that these give you.

You have chosen not to walk away from our relationship, and have been harassing me now for almost eight years. I have been assisting you where I can, but I now understand that the longer I help you, the longer you are going to be an anchor around my neck.

I enabled your behaviour by taking responsibility for your actions. You never suffered the consequences of anything you did, and therefore felt it was my duty to bail you out of everything. I did this because I loved you.

I am tired and worn out; more mentally than physically.

Every relationship in your life is either fake or shallow, depending what you are looking to gain from it. One thing that does not form a part of your relationships is love. Someone without a conscience can't show empathy toward others, and therefore can't express love. Looking back at our initial meeting, it is quite clear that I was targeted as your next victim.

'Sorry' is just a word to you. It holds absolutely no meaning. I am tired of hearing you say sorry on a daily basis.

No more!

I still can't wrap my head around the fact that you preferred lying rather than telling the truth so that we could work things out.

Your lying has become such a part of your life that you are finding it difficult to distinguish between reality and fantasy.

You have become bored with me, and as such, I am walking away.

I sincerely hope that whoever you con into a relationship next time, has more sense than I had and walks away as soon as the real you surfaces.

I don't wish you on anybody.

Good bye,
Wayne

10

MY EXIT STRATEGIES

The tricky part is making a list of exactly what is needed to walk away from someone you love for the sake of your sanity.

You are going to find that most of what you need to do is change your mindset, rather than actual physical actions.

The only physical action that you need to take is to get away from your abuser, and hopefully, you started working out an exit strategy when you realised your relationship was nowhere near normal.

Mentally, you are going to struggle for a very long time after you break off your relationship.

Due to the mental state you find yourself in at the point of walking away, your first thoughts are going to be to convince yourself once again that things will get better.

If that doesn't keep you in the relationship, then the fear of what your partner may do in retribution for you leaving will be the clincher.

This happened too many times for me to be able to count.

Something else that is going to weigh on your mind is your obsession with your partner.

You are going to wonder what she is up to now that you aren't together any longer.

When you were together, she was the only thing on your mind. This doesn't bode well for your mental state now that you are separated.

You are going to worry about how she is coping without you, even though she would have forgotten you the minute she realised and accepted that it was finally over.

She'll move on without blinking an eye; give her a taste of the same.

Even though you are well aware that you were a victim of an emotional abuser, you are going to feel incredibly sad at the breakup of the relationship.

You are in all likelihood going to remember her sob stories as to why she behaves as she does.

These memories of her struggles before she met you, true or false, are going to pull you back towards her.

This is a lasting after-effect of emotional abuse. You keep thinking about what your abuser wants and feels, and your needs become non-existent.

I was, after all, trained by my abuser to think only of her.

Stop obsessing about your abuser and think about yourself.

Start thinking about getting back to the person you were before this episode took hold of your life; reclaim yourself.

If there is one thing you do once you have separated, it is to have NO CONTACT with your abuser.

I understand this may be difficult if there are children involved, but you have to do your best. In this case, keep the contact to the absolute minimum. Don't forget what your ex did to you.

I found that each time I heard my ex's voice or received a message once we had broken up, I still had deep feelings for her.

It didn't matter that most of the messages were threatening, I was just happy to have some contact with her again.

This is what she wants. She intends to keep in touch with you because the longer she has this, the more likely you are of going back to her.

Tread lightly!

If I had to summarise, it would go like this:

1. Acknowledge that you are emotionally abused.

2. Put an exit strategy in place: financial, accommodation and have a support structure.

3. Set boundaries as to what you won't accept any longer and stick to them.

4. Walk away once everything is set up and don't look back.

5. Have no contact with your abuser, or the minimum if there are children involved.

6. Take time to sit back and think about why you were forced to walk away.

7. Find someone to talk to (something I haven't done yet but will need to do soon).

8. Don't rush into another relationship.

11

THE AFTERMATH

'Aftermath' automatically makes us think of what has remained after a disastrous event.

This is where you are going to find yourself - in the ruins of an emotionally abusive relationship.

The aftermath you are going to experience is going to exist in your mind, and the challenge of reversing your mindset will take an immense effort on your part, and of those whom you may turn to for help.

A major issue we face during and after an emotionally abusive relationship is the lack of understanding from those closest to us. This is because others find it difficult to understand the mechanics of systematic abuse and manipulation over a period of time.

It is always 'we told you so...', and no further.

Many a time you will be written off by friends and family because of something that happened in your relationship that affected someone on the outside.

Something you might have said or done without realising may have rubbed someone up the wrong way. They will judge you by that one action, even though they know this 'slip-up' was out of character on your part.

People not involved in this type of relationship have no idea how it affects you mentally, and they also have no concept of the lingering after-effects.

It is sad that those people who write you off don't take the time to sit down with you and ask what is happening.

I am not laying the blame for my abusive relationship at the feet of someone who 'told me so'. It is all on myself and my stupidity for not listening to those around me who saw the danger signs.

Countless emotions take a beating while in an emotionally abusive relationship, and this continues long after the relationship comes to an end.

You are going to judge and analyse everything everyone says and does as a method of protecting yourself.

As a direct result of this, something that I am experiencing significant issues with is trust.

This stems from me still coming to terms with who the 'real' person is that I was in a relationship with, not the fairy tale I fell in love with.

I too have lost the trust of myself to make decisions where it comes to relationships.

Do I want to make a go of a new relationship after what I've just been through?

Does everyone interested in me have the same motives as my ex?

The scars from emotional abuse run so deep that they are going to remain with me for quite some time. You can't walk away from this type of relationship and just brush off what you have been through as though it were something ordinary or insignificant.

It is a learning process and I will have to come to terms with it. I will have to see if I can 'unlearn' the defence mechanisms that I may have adopted during my relationship. They may not go down too well with a prospective partner.

As I come to terms with what I have been through, I have to wonder how it is possible that one person can have such a hold over another?

We discussed self-esteem in a previous chapter, but it is important to touch on this again once you have managed to get out of your abusive relationship.

Even though emotional abuse may not leave physical scars on you, it has a significant impact on your self-esteem.

Emotional abuse in its purest form is a direct attack on your self-esteem.

If you had self-esteem issues when you went into a relationship, you need only to imagine the struggles once you get out of the relationship.

Your self-esteem will be destroyed, and this is now the time to sit back and reflect on what you have been through.

Even possible sexual encounters with prospective new partners are something I have avoided for a long time. I am scared that if any relationship takes that one significant step forward, I am going to find myself back in an emotionally abusive relationship.

I am preventing myself from being happy because I was sad for so long.

I don't want to rush into another relationship, nor do I want to end up alone.

Confusion still reigns.

We don't always realise it, but we go through a dark cycle of grief while we are deciding to walk away from a toxic relationship or any relationship for that matter.

The first thing I felt was akin to when my mother died - a prolonged sense of grief at the loss of a loved one. And then the tears started flowing.

Even when all of my tears over the breakup of the relationship had dried up, I still believed that the two of us were made for, and belonged together.

You will often be sitting on your bed and feel as though your entire soul has been ripped out.

It is one of those feelings that comes from so deep within you that it feels as though you are having a strange medical issue and decide to lie down just in case.

I haven't cried like that in many years, and the sense of relief I experienced afterwards caused me to break into laughter at the realisation of how stupid I was during my entire relationship.

You have lived in a state of emotional confusion, but find it impossible to accept that someone who loves you can treat you in such a manner.

This is the main reason that you stick around much longer than you have to. You have genuine feelings for your partner, and you believe she has the same for you, but all she has been doing is moulding and using you since you met.

It took a few years, but eventually, I accepted that my relationship wasn't a normal one.

For some reason I had this stupid notion that things would improve. All I had to do was bring the person I fell in love with back to the surface. There were small things in her behaviour or words that made me feel there was a glimmer of hope to salvage the relationship.

When I came to terms with the fact that nothing was going to come of this, the anger kicked in.

Firstly, at my ex. I thought about how she had been treating me for so long, and secondly at myself for my stupidity. This is the point where you may even use some of her tactics against her to 'see how she likes it.'

One of the first things I did was to tell friends that I couldn't take the nonsense any longer, but never admitted that I was emotionally abused. I was looking for one of two things. Either confirmation that I made the right decision breaking off the relationship, or what I wanted to hear; 'try and give it another go'.

No matter what you hear from those you have confided in, you are going to seek to salvage your relationship.

DO NOT DO IT!

Once you realise that bargaining with your partner is bad for your mental health and a total waste of your time, you are going to feel as low as you have never felt and may even go through a mild bout of depression.

Depression manifests itself in many forms, but I just ate everything in sight.

This led to weight gain and then to my feeling that women wouldn't find me desirable because of my size. Self-confidence is non-existent.

I withdrew from getting involved with anyone of the opposite sex. I had become so afraid of what women are capable of doing concerning the destruction of my life, that I wanted to avoid all personal contact at all costs. Even though this mindset was a result of one destructive long-term relationship, it still had a profound effect on me.

For years I didn't even attempt to make 'advances' on women because of my irrational fear of them. It was as though I had regressed back to a time when we, as young boys, were just starting to realise that girls and boys were different.

Don't tell yourself to 'snap out of it.' You need sufficient time and space to process and accept all you have been through.

Only then did things get a little easier.

Embrace the fact that you were emotionally abused so that you can move forward.

Don't feel hopeless.

The only thing that will ease what you have been through is time; don't rush things.

You need to get back to the person you were before you experienced this abuse, and the only way to do this is to stay away from the individual who altered your reality.

The journey to rediscover yourself is going to be a fun, but difficult one.

You would have discovered what you want after walking away from your relationship, and this is what you are going to regain.

Don't believe the 'bad press' your abuser was piling on you during the relationship.

You are going to have to separate what your partner said to, or about you, from what you truly know about yourself.

You are not that horrible person she said you were during your time together.

We need to get over our 'niceness' and forget about our abuser, and the only way to do this is to go cold-turkey.

Not contacting your ex again is the only proper way to heal yourself.

The main thing to do now is to 'catch a wake-up'.

Too many times we still have feelings for an ex after the relationship has ended, even though they have put you through hell, and we don't want to break off the relationship.

It doesn't matter how good your good times were because, in my experience, there weren't many of those while you were emotionally abused. Just remind yourself of the misery you experienced while you were with her.

You deserve more. Once you have worked through all of your

feelings, alone or with a therapist, you need to put yourself out there in social circles to get back into the game.

Hate is a powerful word and emotion, and something that I have never felt for anyone or anything. I can't even say that I hate my ex; I feel sorry for who she is.

What I am feeling can be more accurately described as indifference.

I have mentioned a few times I think that it is a good idea to speak to a therapist. I haven't done so yet as I believe that I am still working through things by myself before I ask a professional for help.

I am still trying to see if I can work out where everything went so wrong.

One thing I realised to get away from an abuser, you have to make a decision of no return so that you can reboot your evolution before seeking help. There is no looking back once you've reached this point.

At the exact point of making this decision, your relationship ceases to exist.

Don't look for excuses for anything.

You can't go back to that point where you made the wrong decision 'she'll change', and regret the fact that you stuck around for too long.

Don't continually think into the future; 'Things will get better when…' Make them better for yourself now.

You need to start using your strength and change your mindset immediately.

Fight any thoughts that you will have to try and save your relationship. It is over. Accept and embrace it.

Real strength is shown by walking away from an emotionally abusive relationship, not sticking around and learning to live with it.

You are going to feel a numbness that is going to keep all that has happened in your relationship at the fore-front of your mind. You won't want to do anything except feel sorry for yourself.

This is not all bad. Once you have realised what you need to do to move on, the numbness will make much more sense.

Unfortunately, the after-effects of being in an emotionally abusive relationship are not going to disappear magically. You are going to have to work extremely hard to get back to the normal you.

All I can say is thank you to those people who realised there wasn't anything that they could do other than listen as I went through this difficult time.

Use what you have learnt here to create memories in your life, not drama.

DID YOU ENJOY *HEALING FROM EMOTIONAL ABUSE?*

I would like to thank you for purchasing *Healing from Emotional Abuse: A Personal Journey Through a Toxic Relationship.*

What boggles my mind is that you decided to take a chance on a first-time author to purchase a book that deals with a complicated issue that too many of us experience but are too afraid to speak about.

You have allowed me the privilege of calling myself an author, and for this honour, I thank you.

If I managed to increase your understanding of Emotional Abuse just a little, then I feel I have managed to achieve what I set out to do.

Will you be able to take a few minutes and leave a review of this book on Amazon?

Your feedback will help me to hone my writing skills and produce more, and even better books on this subject.